Nick Can Go Fast

by Elizabeth Franco · illustrated by Violet Lemay

Lucy Calkins and Michael Rae-Grant, Series Editors

Nick Can Go Fast
Author: Elizabeth Franco
Series Editors: Lucy Calkins and Michael Rae-Grant

Heinemann
145 Maplewood Avenue, Suite 300
Portsmouth, NH 03801
www.heinemann.com

Cataloging-in-Publication data is on file with the Library of Congress.

ISBN-13: 978-0-325-13808-4

Design and Production: Dinardo Design LLC, Carole Berg, and Rebecca Anderson

Editors: Anna Cockerille and Jennifer McKenna

Illustrations: Violet Lemay

Photographs: p. 32 © Grindstone Media Group/Shutterstock; inside back cover (fin) © Alessandro De Maddalena/Shutterstock; inside back cover (frog) © Kontrastwerk/ Shutterstock.

Manufacturing: Gerard Clancy

Printed in the United States of America on acid-free paper
3 4 5 6 7 8 9 10 MP 28 27 26 25 24 23
January 2023 printing / PO# 4500866707

Contents

Meet...

Nick

Tam

Cass

Nick and Tam Run

"I can run fast!" Nick says.

"I can run SO fast!" Tam says.

"I can run fast too!"

Cass says.

"Not as fast as us," Nick says.

Get set...GO!

Nick runs. Nick is fast.

Tam runs too. Tam is SO fast.

Tam runs past Nick!

Nick runs past Tam!

Huff! Puff!

Nick is hot. Nick is red.

Nick stops for a sip.

Tam is hot too.

Tam stops for a rest.

Cass runs past Nick and Tam.

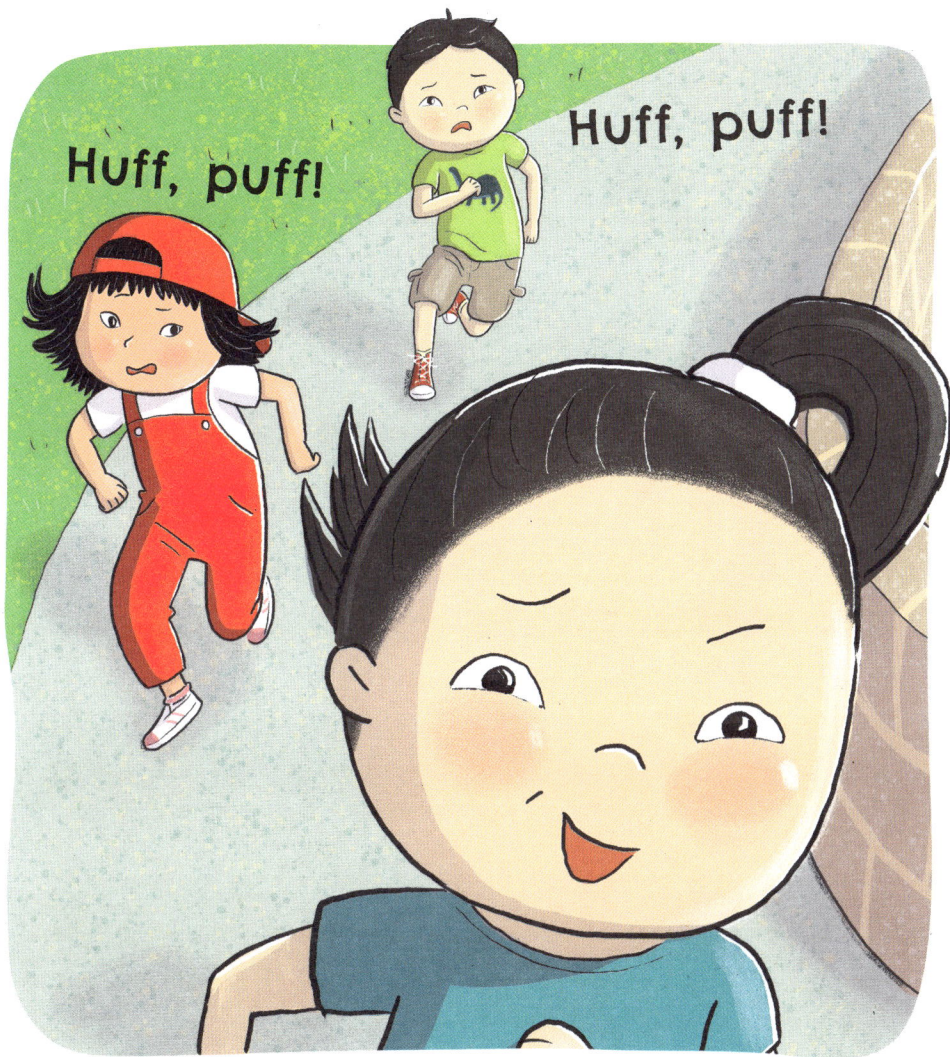

Huff, puff!

Huff, puff!

"See?" says Cass.

"I can run fast too!"

2

The Red Scooter

Nick has a scooter. It is red.

"I like red the best!" says Nick.

Nick is on the ramp.

Nick hits a bump.

Sniff, sniff...

Nick is off the scooter.

Nick gets back on the scooter.

No! A crack!

Nick is off the scooter.

It is NOT fun!

Nick huffs and puffs.

Nick is fed up.

But Nick sees the big kids.

So Nick gets back up.

"I can go fast like the big kids!"
Nick says.

Nick can go fast on
his red scooter.

3

The BIG Truck

Nick can see the BIG truck.

It is so big!

5, 4, 3, 2, 1...GO!

24

The man steps on the gas.

The truck is fast.

The truck puffs.

It gets stuck in the mud.

It can not go.

Rrrrrr!

It spins and spins.

The mud spits at the fans!

"It is SO fun!" Nick says.

MONSTER TRUCKS

Whoa! What is *that* thing flying through the air? It's a *monster truck!* Monster trucks are special trucks that race around a muddy dirt track. *Vroom! Vroom!* Monster trucks are monstrously big. They are 12 feet tall—taller than the ceiling—and they weigh 10,000 pounds. And get this: each wheel on a monster truck is as tall as a grown-up. Even though they're so big and heavy, monster trucks can go very fast. They zoom around the track and up a ramp, then they fly high into the air! Monster trucks can leap over 14 regular cars parked side by side. Check it out!

Sometimes a monster truck lands on a car and then—*CRUNCH!* The monster truck is so heavy that it crushes the car like a soda can. Don't worry—it's an old, broken car, and no one is in it. Lots of people love to watch monster trucks race around a dirt track and crush cars. Would you want to watch that?

Talk about...

Ask your reader some questions like...

- What happened in this book?
- How did Cass win the running race?
- How come Nick was feeling frustrated when he was riding his scooter?

- Nick likes to go fast. He likes to run and ride his scooter. Do you like to go fast?